To Heal Myself

Natalie St John

BookLeaf Publishing

Presentation by *BookLeaf Publishing*

Web: www.bookleafpub.com

E-mail: info@bookleafpub.com

ISBN: 9789357615600

First edition 2022

*I dedicate these poems to my younger self.
I am sorry you lost yourself, but so very
proud of where we are now.*

ACKNOWLEDGEMENT

I would like to thank my friends and family that have helped me through the most transitional period of my life.

PREFACE

In the past 4 years, I have gone through heartbreak, moving back to my hometown, meeting my fiance, and starting our family. These poems helped me get a lot of these feelings off my chest and heal.

I Hope You See Me

I hope you see me
I hope you see the life I have made
the one said wasn't possible without you in it
I hope you see the family I have created
the one that doesn't have you in it
I hope you see the home that I have built
one filled with happiness and love
I hope you see me

Loosing yourself

It doesn't always happen fast
the changes are subtle and small
sometimes you don't even notice
too close to see what's wrong
until one day it hits you
and you notice things have changed
you wonder why it took so long
to see how far you fell

All The Pieces

Let me tell you about a girl
who didn't know who she was
so she copied little bits she liked
from all those that she met
she would take the little pieces
and tie them to herself
sew them together
until she was proud of herself
and when someone didn't like a piece
she would easily throw it away
replace it with the next nice piece
she would find along the way
then the pieces became heavy
all the things that weren't her
started to become hard to carry
weighing in on her
one day they became too much to bare
too hard and heavy to carry
she had to choose between them
all those pieces or herself
so she let them all go
let them slip through her fingers like sand
until all that was left was truly hers
ready for her own pieces

It Didn't Happen That Way

In my mind, I know what's true
my thoughts and feelings
I will bring up the courage to tell you
yet you say it didn't happen that way
you say it with such conviction
I try and stand my ground
but you tell me that it's different
so I start to change my mind
I suppose I am mistaken
that I wasn't exactly right
my mind is so confused
but it's not worth the fight

What You Liked

5

You liked me for a reason
I was small and easy to shape
not yet smart enough to know my worth
you like me for those reasons
it's easy to keep someone like that happy
the bare minimum will do
just enough to keep me distracted
do this long enough
I'll no longer know the difference

The Darkness

I had crawled into the darkness
content with staying there
to sit with all my sorrow
they tried to pull me out
made the light seem so appealing
but I was content in my darkness
it sheltered me from more hurt
cradled me in sadness
whispered that I belonged

Realization

7

I spent so many years not knowing
that what I had was not meant for me
grasping at a rope slipping through my fingers
wondering why my palms were raw

Jump

8

I would have jumped head first
given you every part of me
but you knew that wasn't right
you showed me that I needed to find myself
led me to the field and told me to search
so I looked through the weeds and trees
until I found all the pretty flowers

They waited

9

They were waiting for me
waiting for the time that would learn to let go
to slow down
once I learned this
the world fell into place
my cup was never empty
they were waiting to pour it out
giving me everything I had wanted

The Sunrise After The Storm

The sky begins to lighten
hues of orange and pink
and the warmth touches your skin
you remember what it was like
to bask in the light
almost forgot the feeling in all the rain

Independent

She is independent so she is ok
she can handle it
she can handle the extra weight
carry the extra burden
take it off your plate
it's ok you can give it to her
she will carry it with a smile
never once complain to anyone but herself

Drowning

12

I can be drowning and no one knows it
drowning and no one will see it
but how could they
when my answer is always I'm fine

I Have Waited

I have waited so long for you
prayed to the moon and stars for you
hoping that you would come
and when the years started to slip by
doubt crept into my mind
thinking it was me that was wrong
maybe it wasn't time
or that it wasn't meant for me
so I started to lose hope
kept you in the back of my mind
far enough to dull the ache of your absence
yet close enough to know you may still come

The Light

I carry a small ray of light
in the palm of my hands
a small ray of light amidst the darkness
darkness no one else can see
at times this blackness closes in
and no one else can feel it
but I remember the ray of light
tiny and warm inside my hands

Cut

There's a line across my body
I can't feel it when I touch it
a constant reminder of what happened
its dull ache I constantly feel
I never thought it would take this long
for it to finally heal
part of me hates it
can't stand to look at it
knowing it will never go away

This body

Be proud of what your body has done
be proud of what it has accomplished
but I no longer know this body
everything has changed.

Your Shield

17

I am so excited for your life
for everything that will come your way
I wish you all the happiness
holding your hand along the way
some days I know will be hard
and I will wish to shield your heart
but my love that's not how it works

I will teach you

I will teach you about the trees
about all the flowers and the bees
about the moss, mushrooms, and deer
and all the animals that live in the forest
I will teach you about the world
and hope that you find its beauty
for it holds so much

Printed in the USA
CPSIA information can be obtained
at www.ICGtesting.com
LVHW011204291024
795100LV00015B/719